What is the
Eucharist?

Annemarie
Thimons

Illustrated by
Nancy Rosato–Nuzzo

What is the Eucharist?
Curious Little Catholic Series
Annemarie Thimons

Illustrated by Nancy Rosato–Nuzzo

For additional inspirational books visit us at CuriousLittleCatholic.com

Author's Note:

———◆———

There are many facets of our Catholic faith that are difficult for pre-schoolers to understand. These books have been written as enrichment for the littlest, yet curious, young Catholic children. Should you desire, the scripture verses accompanying each page can be easily memorized by young children. We hope the memorization of these key verses will help strengthen the child's foundation when later studying apologetics. We hope these books will be a beautiful addition to the bookshelves of families who are striving to build homes that foster vocations.

Totus Tuus!

The Eucharist is the center of our faith as Catholics. It is the Body, Blood, Soul, and Divinity of Jesus Christ, given to us under the appearance of bread.

"Jesus said to them, 'I am the bread of life; whoever comes to me will never hunger, and who believes in me will never thirst.'"
John 6:35

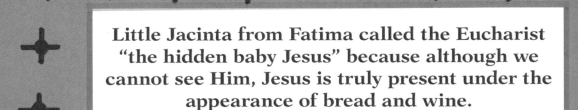

Little Jacinta from Fatima called the Eucharist "the hidden baby Jesus" because although we cannot see Him, Jesus is truly present under the appearance of bread and wine.

"Blessed are those who have not seen and have believed."
John 20:29

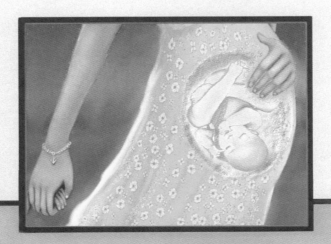

It is like when a Mother is pregnant with a little baby. We cannot see the baby in her belly, but the baby is still there, it is real, and it is alive.

"Amen, amen I say to you, whoever believes has eternal life."
John 6:47

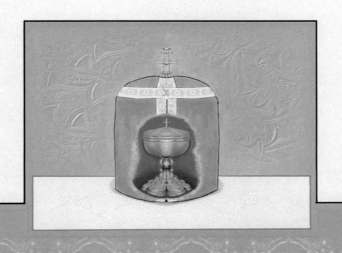

We cannot see Jesus with our eyes in the Eucharist, but He is still there and He is real, and He is alive. This is the greatest gift in the world! To receive Jesus in the Eucharist!

"I am the living bread that came down from heaven, who ever eats this bread will live forever."
John 6:51

Sometimes the Eucharist may be placed in a monstrance on the altar for adoration. Adoration is when we spend time visiting the hidden Jesus.

"Whoever eats my flesh and drinks my blood has eternal life, and I will raise him on the last day."
John 6:54

It brings Jesus such joy to have visitors! We visit the people we love. He also loves us very much and takes care of our souls. We should visit Jesus as often as we can.

*"Look at the birds in the sky; they do not sow or reap,
they gather nothing into barns, yet your heavenly Father feeds them.
Are you not more important than they?"
Matthew 7:26*

When the hidden Jesus in the Eucharist is not at Mass, or in adoration in a monstrance, He stays in the Tabernacle behind the altar. The Tabernacle is a very holy house for our hidden Jesus, where He stays waiting for us.

"For behold I am with you always, until the end of time."
Matthew 28:20

We should always genuflect and make the sign of the cross when we pass the Tabernacle. When we do this, it is our way of saying hello and good bye to our hidden Jesus. We are so blessed to be Catholic and to have the gift of the hidden Jesus in the Eucharist!

"Remain faithful to what you have learned and believed, because you know from whom you learned it."
2 Timothy 3:14

About the Author:

Annemarie (Nuzzo) Thimons is a graduate of Mother of Divine Grace Homestudy and Franciscan University of Steubenville. The Curious Catholic Series was inspired by her five children, whom she and her husband Tom homeschool in New York. She is blessed to have her mother, Nancy, illustrating the stories. She would love to hear stories of sharing the Curious Little Catholic series in your home: www.curiouslittlecatholic.com

About the Illustrator:

Nancy Rosato-Nuzzo, is a freelance illustrator currently working in the beautiful Hudson Valley, New York. A graduate of Long Island University School of the Arts, she is a mixed-media artist who is inspired by the divinity she sees concealed within the daily cadence of life. When she is not in her studio, this mother of three, grandmother of 9, enjoys cooking, gardening, and listening to the music of her husband of 36 years. She is delighted to be collaborating with her daughter on this project.

Made in the USA
Middletown, DE
16 August 2021